Eileen Dunlop and Antony K...

Kings and Queens of Scotland

Illustrated by Maureen and Gordon Gray

Richard Drew Publishing, Glasgow

✽✦✽✦✽✦✽✦✽✦✽✦✽✦✽✦✽✦✽✦✽✦✽✦✽✦✽✦✽✦✽✦✽

✽✦✽✦✽✦✽✦✽✦✽✦✽✦✽✦✽✦✽✦✽✦✽✦✽✦✽✦✽✦✽✦✽

British Library Cataloguing in Publication Data

Dunlop, Eileen
Kings and queens of Scotland.
1. Scotland – Kings and rulers –
Juvenile literature
I. Title   II. Kamm, Antony
941.1'009'92   DA758.2

ISBN 0–86267–063–2
ISBN 0–86267–055–1 Pbk

First Published 1984 by Richard Drew Publishing Ltd,
6 Clairmont Gardens, Glasgow G3 7LW

Copyright © 1984 Eileen Dunlop and Antony Kamm

Designed by James W. Murray
Printed and bound in Great Britain
Set in VIP Pontiff by John Swain Ltd, Glasgow

The First King of Scotland

The Romans came to Scotland, nearly two thousand years ago. They came as invaders, marching in their thousands from the south along the straight stone roads that they had built. They meant to keep what they conquered. Wherever they went, they built forts, each strong enough to withstand fierce attack and supplied with food to last a year.

The native tribes were wild and warlike, but none of them could stand against the disciplined and trained soldiers of Rome. However, in 84 AD, the tribes managed to form themselves into a single force. There was a massive battle at a hill called Mons Graupius. Time and again the tribesmen tried to break the Roman lines, only to be cut down and killed or put to flight.

The Romans never finished conquering Scotland. In time they retreated beyond the defensive wall that their Emperor Hadrian ordered to be built right across Britain from the Tyne to the Solway Firth, and left the peoples of the north to fight among themselves. In about 500 AD two peoples occupied the lands above the Firth of Forth and the Firth of Clyde. Around

Argyll was the kingdom of Dalriada, which belonged to a people from Ireland who called themselves Scots. The rest of the country was held by the Picts.

In those times life was short and often brutal. Both peoples had ways of choosing a successor to their King who would not be a child. A king of Dalriada was succeeded by the eldest, or most able, of his male relations. This heir was chosen by the chief lords while the King was still alive. Among the Picts, a king had to be a son of the line of 'royal women'. He could be succeeded by his brother (that is by his royal mother's son) or by his sister's son, but never by his own son.

For three hundred years the Picts fought against the Scots, and both fought against the peoples to the south. Then came a new menace – the Norsemen. They sailed across the cold North Sea in their longships in search of plunder. They raided churches and monasteries and carried off the treasures that were kept there. They founded settlements in Orkney and Shetland. They even landed in force to do battle with the Picts and the Scots.

During one of these campaigns by the Norsemen both Alpin, King of the Scots, and Eoganan, King of the Picts, were killed in battle. Shortly after that we hear of Kenneth MacAlpin (which means 'son of Alpin') becoming King of the Picts and the Scots together. We do not know how he achieved this. Some say he was related to Eoganan and had a claim to the Pictish throne through one of the line of royal women. Others say he got it by treachery. However he did it, he defended the new kingdom, which became known as Scotia, vigorously against the Norsemen and against invaders from the south, and led six expeditions into England. He made Scone in Perthshire his chief town, and he was proclaimed King on the ancient Stone of Destiny. He moved the relics of the holy St Columba from the island of Iona to a new church which he built at Dunkeld. Kenneth I ruled for 16 years. He died in 859 not in battle, nor by murder, but from a tumour. According to the law of the Scots he was succeeded by his brother, Donald I, though two of his sons, Constantine I and Aed, became Kings of Scotia later.

3

	Born	Reigned	
1 **KENNETH I** (MacAlpin)	?	843–859	First King of the Picts and the Scots. (See page 2)
2 **DONALD I**	?	859–863	Brother of Kenneth I.
3 **CONSTANTINE I**	?	863–877	Nephew of Donald I and son of Kenneth I. Killed in battle against the Norsemen.
4 **AED**	?	877–878	Brother of Constantine I. Killed by his cousin Giric.
5 **EOCHAID**	?	878–889	Nephew of Aed and grandson of Kenneth I. Ruled jointly with Giric.
6 **DONALD II**	?	889–900	Cousin of Eochaid and son of Constantine I.
7 **CONSTANTINE II**	?	900–943	First cousin of Donald II and son of Aed. Abdicated and went into a monastery. Died 952.
8 **MALCOLM I**	?	943–954	Cousin of Constantine II and son of Donald II. Took Moray into his kingdom but was killed in a rebellion there.
9 **INDULF**	?	954–962	Cousin of Malcolm I and son of Constantine II. Took Edinburgh into his kingdom. Killed by the Norsemen.
10 **DUFF (or DUBH, 'The Black')**	?	962–966	Cousin of Indulf and son of Malcolm I. Defeated and killed by Colin, Indulf's son.
11 **COLIN (or CULEN, 'The Whelp')**	?	966–971	Cousin of Duff and son of Indulf. Killed by the King of Strathclyde, whose daughter he had seized.
12 **KENNETH II**	?	971–995	Cousin of Colin and brother of Duff. Killed in a blood feud.
13 **CONSTANTINE III**	?	995–997	Cousin of Kenneth II and son of Colin. Killed by Malcolm, Kenneth II's son.
14 **KENNETH III, 'The Grim'**	?	997–1005	Cousin of Constantine III and son of Duff. Killed by his successor Malcolm, Kenneth II's son.
15 **MALCOLM II**	945*	1005–1034	Cousin of Kenneth III and son of Kenneth II. Took Lothian and Strathclyde into his kingdom. Last King of the line of Alpin.
16 **DUNCAN I**	1001*	1034–1040	Grandson of Malcolm II by a daughter. Killed in battle against Macbeth. (See page 7)
17 **MACBETH**	1005*	1040–1057	Cousin of Duncan I and grandson of Kenneth II. Killed in battle against Malcolm III. (See page 7)
18 **LULACH, 'The Simple'**	1032*	1057–1058	Stepson of Macbeth and great-grandson of Kenneth III. Killed by Malcolm III.
19 **MALCOLM III, 'Canmore'**	1031*	1058–1093	Son of Duncan I. Killed in an attack upon England. (See page)
20 **DONALD III, 'Donald Bane'**	1033*	1093–1097	Brother of Malcolm III. Defeated by Duncan II, eldest son of Malcolm III, who was killed in a revolt in Moray shortly afterwards. Donald became King again, but was finally defeated by Edgar, blinded and imprisoned.
21 **DUNCAN II**	1060*	May-Nov 1094	
22 **EDGAR**	1074*	1097–1107	Half-brother of Duncan II and son Malcolm III. Died unmarried.
23 **ALEXANDER I, 'The Fierce'**	1076*	1107–1124	Brother of Edgar. Died childless.
24 **DAVID I, 'The Saint'**	1080*	1124–1153	Brother of Alexander I. Strengthen the Church and encouraged Norm to settle in Scotland.
25 **MALCOLM IV, 'The Maiden'**	1142	1153–1165	Grandson of David I. Died unmarried.
26 **WILLIAM I, 'The Lion'**	1143	1165–1214	Brother of Malcolm IV. Bought b the independence of Scotland aft being defeated and captured by English.
27 **ALEXANDER II**	1198	1214–1249	Son of William I. Died on board s while trying to take the Hebrides f. Norway.
28 **ALEXANDER III**	1241	1249–1286	Son of Alexander II. Died from a f (See page 9)
* About.			

Queens of Scotland

	Born	Reigned	
MARGARET, 'The Maid of Norway'	1283	1286–1290	Granddaughter of Alexander III. (See page 10)
JOHN (Balliol)	1249	1292–1296	Descendant of David I. Abdicated. Died in 1315. (See page 10)
ROBERT I, 'The Bruce'	1274	1306–1329	Descendant of David I. (See page 10)
DAVID II	1324	1329–1371	Son of Robert I and his second wife, Elizabeth. Spent 11 years as a prisoner of the English. Died childless.
ROBERT II (Stewart)	1316	1371–1390	Nephew of David II and grandson of Robert I by his daughter. The first Stewart King and the oldest who ever ruled Scotland.
ROBERT III (Stewart)	1337*	1390–1406	Son of Robert II and Elizabeth Mure. Changed his name from John since that name was associated with unlucky Kings.
JAMES I (Stewart)	1394	1406–1437	Son of Robert III and Annabella Drummond. Murdered at Perth. (See page 14)
JAMES II (Stewart)	1430	1437–1460	Son of James I and Joan Beaufort. Killed at Roxburgh Castle by an explosion. (See page 16)
JAMES III (Stewart)	1451	1460–1488	Son of James II and Mary of Gueldres. Murdered near Stirling. (See page 17)
JAMES IV (Stewart)	1473	1488–1513	Son of James III and Margaret of Denmark. Killed at the Battle of Flodden. (See page 18)
JAMES V (Stewart)	1512	1513–1542	Son of James IV and Margaret Tudor. Died at Falkland Palace. (See page 20)
MARY (Stuart†), 'Queen of Scots'	1542	1542–1567	Daughter of James V and Mary of Guise. Abdicated. Executed in England, 1587. (See page 22)
JAMES VI (Stuart)	1566	1567–1625	Son of Mary and her second husband Henry Stuart, Lord Darnley. Became James I of England in 1603. (See page 24)
CHARLES I (Stuart)	1600	1625–1649	Son of James VI and Anne of Denmark. Executed by the English Parliament. (See page 26)

† This is the French way of spelling Stewart, which Mary adopted.

	Born	Reigned	
43 **CHARLES II** (Stuart)	1630	1649–1685	Son of Charles I and Henrietta Maria of France. Restored to the English throne in 1660. (See page 27)
44 **JAMES VII** (Stuart)	1633	1685–1688	James II of England. Brother of Charles II. Abdicated. Died in France in 1701. (See page 28)
45 **WILLIAM** (of Orange)	1650	1689–1702	Grandson of Charles I by his daughter.
and **MARY** (Stuart)	1662	1689–1694	Daughter of James VII and Anne Hyde. She and William had no children. (See page 29)
46 **ANNE** (Stuart)	1665	1702–1714	Sister of Mary. Married to Prince George of Denmark. She died childless and was the last Stuart monarch. (See page 30)
47 **GEORGE I** (of Hanover)	1660	1714–1727	Great-grandson of James VI. (See page 30)
48 **GEORGE II**	1683	1727–1760	Son of George I and Dorothea of Zell.
49 **GEORGE III**	1738	1760–1820	Grandson of George II. Because of his madness his son became Regent in 1810.
50 **GEORGE IV**	1762	1820–1830	Son of George III and Charlotte Sophia of Mecklenburg-Strelitz. His daughter by his wife, Caroline of Brunswick, died in 1817. (See page 31)
51 **WILLIAM** (IV of England)	1765	1830–1837	Brother of George IV. Neither of his daughters by Adelaide of Saxe-Meiningen survived.
52 **VICTORIA**	1819	1837–1901	Niece of William and granddaughter of George III. (See page 31)
53 **EDWARD** (VII of England)	1841	1901–1910	Son of Victoria and Prince Albert of Saxe-Coburg.
54 **GEORGE V**	1865	1910–1936	Son of Edward and Princess Alexandra of Denmark. (See page 31)
55 **EDWARD** (VIII of England)	1894	Jan-Dec 1936	Eldest son of George V and Princess Mary of Teck. Abdicated. Died in 1972.
56 **GEORGE VI**	1895	1936–1952	Second son of George V.
57 **ELIZABETH**	1926	1952–	Elizabeth II of England. Elder daughter of George VI and Lady Elizabeth Bowes-Lyon.

Genealogical Tree from KENNETH I to ROBERT I

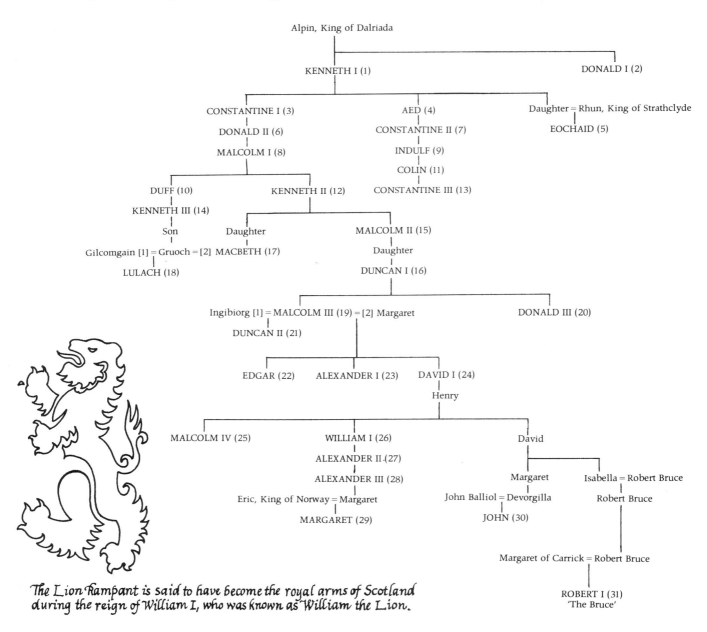

Alpin, King of Dalriada

KENNETH I (1) — DONALD I (2)

CONSTANTINE I (3) — AED (4) — Daughter = Rhun, King of Strathclyde

DONALD II (6) — CONSTANTINE II (7) — EOCHAID (5)

MALCOLM I (8) — INDULF (9)

COLIN (11)

DUFF (10) — KENNETH II (12) — CONSTANTINE III (13)

KENNETH III (14)

Son — Daughter — MALCOLM II (15)

Gilcomgain [1] = Gruoch = [2] MACBETH (17) — Daughter

LULACH (18) — DUNCAN I (16)

Ingibiorg [1] = MALCOLM III (19) = [2] Margaret — DONALD III (20)

DUNCAN II (21)

EDGAR (22) ALEXANDER I (23) DAVID I (24)

Henry

MALCOLM IV (25) WILLIAM I (26) David

ALEXANDER II (27)

ALEXANDER III (28) Margaret Isabella = Robert Bruce

Eric, King of Norway = Margaret John Balliol = Devorgilla Robert Bruce

MARGARET (29) JOHN (30)

Margaret of Carrick = Robert Bruce

ROBERT I (31)
'The Bruce'

The Lion Rampant is said to have become the royal arms of Scotland during the reign of William I, who was known as William the Lion.

Macbeth
(1040–1057)

Malcolm II, fifteenth King of Scotia, reigned for thirty years, during which he enlarged the kingdom to include Lothian and Strathclyde. He had no sons, but he wanted his grandson Duncan to succeed him. To make sure, he murdered one of the chief claimants to the throne.

In Shakespeare's play 'Macbeth' and in some story-books, you will read that Duncan was a gracious old man who was foully murdered by the tyrant Macbeth and that Macbeth then seized the throne from Duncan's son, Malcolm.

In fact Duncan and Macbeth, who were cousins, were both quite young men. Under Scots law Macbeth had as much claim to the throne as Duncan, for he is said to have been a grandson of Kenneth II. His wife was of the royal line too, for she was a granddaughter of Kenneth III. Macbeth was ruler of the district of Moray. He started a rebellion against Duncan. Duncan took an army to Moray to seek him out, but was defeated and killed by Macbeth in battle. Malcolm was only nine at the time, and was too young to be King.

Macbeth was called 'the fierce red one' and he seems to have been a good king. During his reign Scotland prospered and grew rich. Macbeth and his wife granted lands to a community of monks. He went on a pilgrimage to Rome, where he threw money to the poor. Duncan's father, Crinan, tried to raise a rebellion against Macbeth, but he was beaten in battle and killed too. Then the King of England sent an army under Earl Siward to put young Malcolm on the Scottish throne. Siward defeated Macbeth's army and pushed it right back beyond the Forth, whereupon Malcolm proclaimed himself King in southern Scotland. Then he went after Macbeth himself. Between Birnam Wood and Dunsinane Hill (by Perth), on which was Macbeth's castle, their soldiers fought and Macbeth was put to flight. Three years later, at Lumphanan, which is 25 miles west of Aberdeen, Macbeth made his last stand. Today a cairn marks where his body was buried for a short time before it could be taken for royal burial on Iona.

Malcolm III
(1058–1093)

Even when Macbeth was dead, Malcolm was not properly King of Scotland. Some people preferred Lulach, Macbeth's stepson. So Malcolm had Lulach ambushed and killed. Only then could he truly call himself King. Malcolm's nickname was Canmore, which means 'the big-headed'. Though he spoke English, Latin and Gaelic, he could not read or write. He was a warrior, and he wanted to enlarge his kingdom.

Malcolm invaded Northumberland in England and killed those whom he could not bring back as slaves. In return the English King, William the Conqueror, came north, made Malcolm submit to him, and took Malcolm's eldest son Duncan back with him as a hostage. Malcolm still would not keep the peace. Twice more he invaded England, killing and plundering: each time the English returned and forced him to make peace. Yet in 1093 Malcolm tried again. With his son Edward, he was ambushed and killed by the Earl of Northumberland. Two Englishmen buried Malcolm: twenty years later his body was dug up and brought back to Dunfermline Abbey to lie beside that of his Queen Margaret.

Margaret (she later became St Margaret) was Malcolm's second wife. She was a princess of the old royal line of England which had been pushed aside by William the Conqueror. She was a very religious person, who persuaded Malcolm that many of the old customs of the Church in Scotland should be changed to make them like Christian practices elsewhere. She built churches and monasteries. She and Malcolm turned the fort on the rock at Edinburgh into a royal castle, filled it with rich hangings and furniture, and made there the tiny chapel which today still bears her name. She was lying ill when her eldest son Edgar came to tell her that Malcolm and Edward were dead. She died four days later. As her body lay in her chapel, Malcolm's brother Donald Bane was proclaiming himself the new King of Scotland and was laying siege to the Castle. Under cover of mist, Margaret's servants stole out with the coffin and ferried it across the Forth to Dunfermline.

Alexander III
(1249–1286)

Alexander III became King when he was seven years old. At ten, he was married to the daughter of King Henry III of England. That meant peace with England. In 1263, at the Battle of Largs, he managed to prevent a huge sea-force of Norsemen from invading Scotland. He made a treaty with the Norsemen and, to ensure that the peace would be kept, he married his daughter to the King of Norway.

Alexander was a man of peace. In peacetime people can get on with their own work. Though some people spoke English, some French and some Gaelic, and could not understand each other; and though the Highlanders were very different from the farmers and the traders in the south of the country, for the first time the people of Scotland began to regard themselves as belonging to one nation. There were no serious rebellions. In any case Alexander's lords used the times of peace to make their castles really secure.

However, there was much sadness for Alexander. In 1275 his wife died, and then his only two sons. He badly wanted a son to succeed him. He married a beautiful French woman called Yolande, hoping that she would give him a son. One dark and stormy night he left Edinburgh, crossed the Forth by the ferry, and rode off ahead of his servants to the royal manor at Kinghorn to be with his wife. He never arrived. The next morning his body was found at the foot of a cliff. He was only 44. He had reigned for 36 years, and he had been married to Queen Yolande for just six months.

After Bruce's coronation, Edward I took cruel revenge. He had Bruce's wife and daughter shut up in separate prisons. He hanged Bruce's brother. He took his sister and the brave Countess of Buchan, who had placed the crown on Bruce's head, and imprisoned them in cages.

Robert the Bruce
(1306–1329)

Alexander III's only living relation now was his little granddaughter, the 'Maid of Norway'. The Scottish nobles sent for her to come and be Queen. She died on the voyage. Thirteen men then claimed they had a right to the throne. When they could not decide between them who should be the King, they asked Edward I, King of England, to choose for them. Edward had long wanted to rule Scotland as well as England and Wales. So he chose John Balliol, a weak man, who could be made to do what Edward wanted. In 1296, Balliol gave up the throne. Scotland now had no king. For a time William Wallace governed the country, calling himself Guardian of Scotland. He fought the English valiantly until he was betrayed, captured and taken to London for execution.

The two leading men in Scotland were now John Comyn and Robert the Bruce, who was grandson of one of the thirteen who had claimed the throne before. Bruce had an argument with Comyn in a church and stabbed him to death. This was a terrible crime. The only way that Bruce could avoid being made an outlaw and at the same time free his country from the rule of England, was to have himself crowned King.

At first only a few would follow him. He could not risk battle, so he set ambushes and made surprise attacks from the hills. After one skirmish he and a companion were pursued by five Highlanders. Bruce killed four of them, and his companion the other. The very next morning Bruce woke up to see three men coming at him with drawn swords. He killed them too.

Edward I, for his warlike deeds and his cruelty, was called 'The Hammer of the Scots'. When he died, he asked his son Edward II to put his bones in a box and carry them to Scotland at the head of his troops. However, Edward felt he was too busy for the moment to attack Scotland. All this time more and more men were joining Bruce, fired by his exploits, though he still did not have enough to take on the whole English army. Then the fateful time came when he had to do so. His brother had accepted the offer of the Governor of Stirling Castle to surrender if the English did not come to relieve it before next mid-summer's day, 24 June 1314. Stirling was a vital fortress, for it guarded the main route between the north and south of Scotland. Bruce had to have the Castle: if necessary, he would fight for it.

On 23 June, Bruce saw the English approaching – 15,000 foot-soldiers, including archers, and 3000 heavy cavalry. He had only 8000 men in all, and his 500 horsemen were only lightly armed. The Battle of Bannockburn started with a disaster for the English. One of their knights, Sir Henry de Bohun, charged at Bruce with his lance. Bruce, who had only a battle-axe, calmly swerved his horse aside and with one blow shattered de Bohun's skull.

The next day Bruce sent his spearmen, in close-packed order, straight against the English cavalry, and ordered his horsemen to attack the archers who were firing into his men from the side. His tactics succeeded brilliantly. The English were put to flight.

Scotland was now free of English control. However, it took another 14 years of Scottish raids into England before the young King Edward III agreed to sign a treaty recognising Scotland as an independent country and Bruce as her King. The next year Bruce died. But he had achieved what he had fought for.

What finally won the Battle of Bannockburn for the Scots was the sudden appearance of fresh troops who charged down a hill, shouting and screaming. The English panicked, thinking that a whole new Scottish army was attacking them. In fact, it was simply a band of 'small folk', untrained followers of the Scottish army whom Bruce had kept back from the battle until then.

Genealogical Tree from ROBERT I

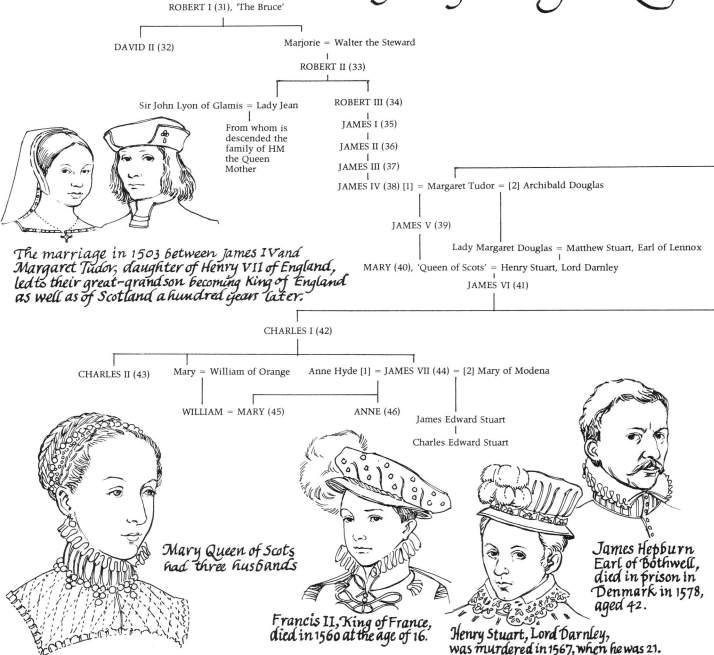

ROBERT I (31), 'The Bruce'

DAVID II (32)

Marjorie = Walter the Steward

ROBERT II (33)

Sir John Lyon of Glamis = Lady Jean

From whom is descended the family of HM the Queen Mother

ROBERT III (34)

JAMES I (35)

JAMES II (36)

JAMES III (37)

JAMES IV (38) [1] = Margaret Tudor = [2] Archibald Douglas

JAMES V (39)

Lady Margaret Douglas = Matthew Stuart, Earl of Lennox

MARY (40), 'Queen of Scots' = Henry Stuart, Lord Darnley

JAMES VI (41)

CHARLES I (42)

CHARLES II (43)   Mary = William of Orange   Anne Hyde [1] = JAMES VII (44) = [2] Mary of Modena

WILLIAM = MARY (45)   ANNE (46)

James Edward Stuart

Charles Edward Stuart

The marriage in 1503 between James IV and Margaret Tudor, daughter of Henry VII of England, led to their great-grandson becoming King of England as well as of Scotland a hundred years later.

Mary Queen of Scots had three husbands

Francis II, King of France, died in 1560 at the age of 16.

Henry Stuart, Lord Darnley, was murdered in 1567, when he was 21.

James Hepburn Earl of Bothwell, died in prison in Denmark in 1578, aged 42.

o the Present Day

Henry VII of England
    Henry VIII
Mary Tudor   Elizabeth   Edward VI

Queen Anne, whose husband was Prince George of Denmark, was the last Stuart monarch.

Elizabeth = Frederick, King of Bohemia
    Sophia = Ernest Augustus, Elector of Hanover
        GEORGE I (47)
        GEORGE II (48)
    Frederick, Prince of Wales
        GEORGE III (49)
GEORGE IV (50)   WILLIAM IV (51)   Edward = Victoria of Saxe-Coburg
                        VICTORIA (52)
                    EDWARD VII (53)
                    GEORGE V (54)
Lady Elizabeth Bowes-Lyon = GEORGE VI (56)   EDWARD VIII (55)
(HM the Queen Mother)
            ELIZABETH (57)

After the death of Queen Anne in 1714, the crown passed to the descendants of Elizabeth (1596-1662), sister of Charles I and daughter of James VI. She married the King of Bohemia and was known as the Winter Queen.

James I
(1406–1437)

Robert the Bruce's son, David II, died childless. The heir was Robert II, son of Bruce's daughter Marjorie. He was the first King of the line of the Stewarts, who were to rule Scotland for nearly 350 years, and England too for 111 of them. The family originally came from France, possibly with William the Conqueror. One of them was later rewarded by David I with the title of hereditary High Steward (or Stewart) of Scotland. Marjorie was married to the sixth High Steward.

James I was a Stewart and great-great-grandson of Bruce. When he was 11 his father, Robert III, fearful for his safety, sent him by ship to France. The ship, with James in it, was captured by the English. That same day, Robert III died.

So, the new King of Scotland became a prisoner in the Tower of London. Though later he was allowed out, given a good education and lived at the English court, he remained a prisoner for 18 years. He grew up strong and clever. He was an excellent athlete and also a fine poet – he wrote a beautiful poem called *The Kingis Quair* (which means 'The Book of the King'). He also fell in love, with a high-born English girl, Joan Beaufort, granddaughter of the famous John of Gaunt. James was finally set free in 1424, on condition that the Scots promised to pay £40,000 to cover the cost of his board and lodging while he had been a prisoner! Then he rode north with his Queen, determined to be a firm ruler.

Five days after he was crowned at Scone, James called a meeting of Parliament. He persuaded it to pass laws to prevent rebellions, to stop people fighting each other, and to make sure that the barons did not have too much power or help themselves to money and lands which belonged to the Crown. He ordered Parliament to meet again soon. Then it made laws especially to help the weak get justice against the strong.

Then James moved against his enemies. He ordered the Duke of Albany, who had been Regent of Scotland while James was a prisoner in England, to be tried for treason. Albany was found guilty and he and his two sons were executed. James called

Parliament to meet at Inverness and commanded the Highland chiefs to attend. As they came through the door, they were arrested and thrown into dungeons, while James amused his barons by reciting Latin verses which he had made up. Some of the chiefs were hanged immediately; some were tried, found guilty of various crimes, and beheaded; others he let go free.

Many people hated James. One day, as he and his court were getting on the ferry to cross the Forth, an old woman stopped him. 'I see the shroud across your breast', she said. 'If you cross the water, you will never return.' James took no notice, and went on to Blackfriars Monastery in Perth, where they were all to stay for Christmas.

One night at Perth, James was with the Queen and her ladies, getting ready for bed. There was a clatter of weapons on the stairs outside. They rushed to the door. The lock had been removed and the bar to go through the staples to bolt the door was missing. James remembered that under the floor of the chamber was a tunnel. It led nowhere now. It used to have an opening into an indoor tennis-court but he had had it blocked up because he kept losing balls in it during play. He levered up the floorboards with the fire-tongs and jumped down. As the boards were being put back, the page outside the door screamed. One of the ladies, Kate Douglas, rushed over and thrust her arm through the staples to hold it shut. Several men pushed at the door, shattering the bones in her arm. When they managed to break in, the King was not there. They threatened the Queen, and then went away disgusted.

As the boards were being lifted up to let James out, one fell back with a bang. The men ran back into the room. They saw a hole in the floor, and in it the King. James fought them with his bare hands. When the murderers had finished, he had 28 deep wounds in his body.

James II
(1437–1460)

The murderers of James I were caught and tortured to death. The new King, James II, was only six years old. He was known as 'James of the Fiery Face' because of the great red birthmark on his cheek. Though James I had strengthened the authority of Parliament, the real rulers now were the barons, especially Crichton, Governor of Edinburgh Castle, and Livingstone, Governor of Stirling Castle.

Crichton and Livingstone decided that they must do something about the young Earl of Douglas, whose power they feared. They invited Douglas and his brother to dine with the boy King at Edinburgh Castle. When the meal was finished, the two Douglases were seized, taken outside and beheaded.

When James was 19, and just married, he decided to bring some order to the country himself. He had six leading members of the Livingstone family arrested and tried by Parliament, and all their belongings confiscated. Two of them were executed and the rest imprisoned. However, there was still trouble from the Douglas family. A new Earl of Douglas had made an alliance with other nobles which could be dangerous to the King. James invited Douglas to Stirling Castle. After supper he asked Douglas to break the alliance. Douglas refused. James lost his temper, drew his dagger and stabbed Douglas in the throat. His attendants finished Douglas off with pikes and swords and threw the body out of the window.

James continued to oppress the Douglas family until they were no longer a danger. Then there was peace in Scotland. Parliament passed laws encouraging agriculture and archery, but forbidding football and golf! Ordinary people must dress in grey or white for work, but could wear red, green or light blue on holidays.

When the rebellion known as the War of the Roses broke out in England, James went to help the English King Henry VI. He laid siege to Roxburgh Castle, which was then an English fortress. As he watched the bombardment, one of his cannons exploded. He was hit by a piece of metal, and died instantly.

James III
(1460–1488)

James III was just nine when he was crowned, and for three years until her death his mother, Queen Mary, ruled the country. When he grew up, he married the Danish Princess Margaret, and as part of the arrangement took back Orkney and Shetland, which had been occupied by the Norsemen hundreds of years before. Then he broke the power of the Boyd family, who had been trying to get for themselves the top jobs in the land.

However, James was not liked by his nobles. He was interested in art and architecture and music, and gathered around him men with similar interests, however low-born they might be. He had favourites, to whom he gave rich clothes and expensive presents. At last the nobles decided to ask James's brother, the Duke of Albany, to become King in his place. James heard about the plot and imprisoned Albany in Edinburgh Castle and his brother, the Earl of Mar, in Craigmillar Castle. Albany got his guards drunk, killed them, climbed down the rock-face on a rope, and escaped to England. Mar died in his bath, it is said on the orders of the King.

Albany, with an army given him by the English King, Edward IV, marched north to take the throne of Scotland. James and his army set out to meet him. On the way, James's nobles tried to persuade him to give up his powers to them. When he refused, they seized six of his favourites and hanged them from Lauder Bridge. Then they took James to Edinburgh and put him in the Castle. Albany ruled for a few months, but finally had to give way to James and was banished from the country.

Now the nobles proclaimed the King's eldest son, Prince James, ruler of Scotland. The forces of the King and of the Prince fought at Sauchieburn, and the King fled. His horse threw him, and he was carried to a mill, badly hurt. He called for a priest. The miller's wife ran out and came back with a man who said he was a priest. He knelt beside the King, and stabbed him to death!

James IV
(1488–1513)

James IV was so upset by the way his father died that for the rest of his life he wore an iron chain round his waist, next to the skin. He was 15 when he came to the throne; old enough to be interested in the good of his country.

James was excited by the discoveries and inventions that were being made in Europe. He liked to do things for himself, too. He did experiments in chemistry: he paid people to let him pull out their teeth: he tried being a doctor as well. In 1506 he granted a Royal Charter to the College of Surgeons in Edinburgh. He founded the University of Aberdeen. He encouraged Parliament to pass a law that all 'barons and freeholders' must send their eldest sons to school from the age of nine until they had mastered Latin, and then to spend three years studying languages and law. He introduced printing to Scotland, so that now people could have books which were produced locally. Poetry became a great art in James's reign, and poems by Dunbar and Henryson in particular are read and studied still. He made vast improvements to Stirling Castle and to his palaces at Falkland and Linlithgow. He also turned the guesthouse of the Abbey of Holyroodhouse into a mighty palace, and built the great north-west tower which still stands today.

James IV determined also that there should be peace in Scotland and that, if he had to go to war, his army and navy would be properly equipped. Six times he visited the Western Isles, at first in force but later welcomed as King, until he was satisfied that there would be no trouble from the Highland chiefs. He built a new fleet. We read that all the woods in Fife were chopped down (except Falkland Wood – presumably that would have spoilt the King's hunting) to go to the making of the 'Great Michael', the biggest and most heavily armed warship in the world. He brought armourers from France to construct great cannons in Edinburgh Castle.

James's marriage to Margaret Tudor, daughter of King Henry VII of England, was a splendid affair. Though James was

said never to cut his red hair or to shave, the next morning he had his beard cut off to please his bride. Then there was a week of celebration, especially the King's favourite sport of jousting. They were married just nine years, during which Margaret had six children, only one of whom survived infancy. But by their marriage, the crowns of Scotland and England were later to be joined.

Though James was married to the sister of Henry VIII, who became King of England in 1509, there came a time when he had to fight England. Scotland had long had a treaty with France that if either country was attacked by England, the other would go to its support. So when in 1513 Henry VIII invaded France, James had no choice. To help France, he invaded England.

The guns were dragged out of Edinburgh Castle. The finest army Scotland had ever seen assembled outside the city. Two weeks later the Scots crossed into England and halted on Flodden Hill. When he saw them, the English commander sent a message to challenge James to fight on 9 September. James accepted.

The night before the battle, it is said that a ghostly herald appeared in the High Street of Edinburgh, crying aloud the names of those who would die on the morrow, ending with the King. The battle started with cannon fire from both sides. The Scottish guns did little damage as they were on the hill and their shots flew over the English lines. Then James ordered his spearmen to attack. Kicking off their shoes to get a firmer grip on the wet ground, they advanced, in total silence. The battle was between two sides of equal numbers. Someone who knew James once said: 'He begins to fight before he has given his orders. He says it would be wrong to go into battle unless he himself was the first man in danger.' That is what happened at Flodden. James, in the front rank, died early on with an arrow in his throat, just a spear's length from the English commander.

The Scots had lost their leader, and their King. They fought on, but many of them were slaughtered where they stood. It was the greatest disaster Scotland had ever known.

James V
(1513–1542)

The new King was a baby of 17 months when he was crowned. Soon afterwards his mother, Queen Margaret, married Archibald Douglas, Earl of Angus, who was grandson of one of the men who had strung up James III's favourites, and a distant cousin of the Douglas whom James II had stabbed at Stirling. Though Margaret soon tired of her new husband and divorced him, Angus got control of the King when James was 14 and kept him in Falkland Palace. He also managed to appoint other members of his own family to high offices.

Two years later James escaped to Stirling, where he was joined by those nobles who wanted to see the end of the Douglas family. James rode with an army to Tantallon Castle, the Douglas stronghold. The Douglases fled to England without a fight. Even so, James continued to take revenge against the family. In 1537 John, Master of Forbes, who was brother-in-law to Angus, was executed for the extraordinary crime of plotting to shoot the King with a cannon. Three days later James allowed Lady Glamis, Angus's sister, to be publicly burned alive for trying to poison him.

James was ruthless to robbers too. Once he was hunting with his followers when John Alexander, a well-known Border cattle-thief, came up to greet him, with 24 of his men. James ordered the lot of them to be hung on the nearest trees. However, James had a kinder side too. He liked to go around the countryside in disguise, calling himself 'The Goodman of Ballengeich'. One day he saw a tinker drinking outside an inn and went and sat down beside him. As they talked, the tinker said he wished he could see the King.

'Come on,' said James. 'Jump up behind me on my horse and we'll go and find him. He's hunting nearby.'

'But how shall I know which is the King among all those smart nobles?' asked the tinker.

'Easy,' replied James. 'He'll be the one with a hat on.'

When they approached the hunting party, everyone took off his hat and bowed to James. Then the tinker realised who his friend was. He jumped to the ground and bowed too.

Henry VIII of England

James V of Scotland

James's Queen, Mary of Guise

In 1536 James was 24 and unmarried. His greatest problem was money. He needed a rich wife who would hopefully also give him a son to succeed him. He married Madeleine, daughter of the King of France, but she died seven weeks after they returned to Scotland. In 1538 he was married again, to a beautiful French widow, Mary of Guise. They had two sons, but both died in 1541. Scotland was without an heir again.

At this time, in Scotland as in the rest of Europe, religious reformers were preaching changes to the accepted way of Catholic worship. France remained strongly Catholic. King Henry VIII of England, who was James's uncle, had broken with the Pope and wanted James to back him up. He also feared an attack from France. James, who had a French wife and needed the money his Catholic bishops gave him, had no intention of becoming Protestant or encouraging his people to do so. Henry invited him to come to York to discuss the matter. James did not turn up. Henry was so furious that to try and get James to understand his way of thinking, he sent a raiding party into Scotland, which was easily defeated and its commander captured.

James now wanted his army to invade England. His nobles refused to lead any such attack. James was losing his grip on the country. He got together another force and appointed his favourite, Oliver Sinclair, as commander. This made the nobles even angrier. Sinclair got his troops in a terrible tangle at the battle called Solway Moss. Many of them surrendered without a fight: others were caught in a bog.

This was too much for James to bear. He retired to Falkland Palace, where he sank into an illness, some say brought on by his melancholy, from which he never recovered. Just before he died, the Queen gave birth to a girl. Scotland had an heir to the throne. When he heard the news, James said: 'It came with a lass: it will end with a lass.' He meant the royal line of the Stewarts, which had begun with Robert the Bruce's daughter, Marjorie. Later in the book we shall see whether James's prophecy about its end was correct.

Mary Queen of Scots

(1542–1567)

John Knox hated Mary because she was Catholic and because she liked to enjoy herself with music and dancing. He was especially angry at the festivities with which the people of Edinburgh greeted her when she arrived. In St Giles' Church he preached sermons against her. Mary called for him to come and see her in the Palace. They argued, and Knox upset her so much that after he left, she burst into tears.

Mary, daughter of James V, was only seven days old when she became Queen. Henry VIII, hoping to unite Scotland with England, proposed that Mary should marry his son Edward. The Scots refused. So Henry sent in troops. The Scots appealed to France for help. The French agreed, if Mary came to France to be the future wife of Francis, heir to the French throne.

Mary was only 16 when she was married – at the wedding feast her crown was so heavy, she had to take it off. Later, news came that Mary Tudor, who had succeeded the sickly Edward on the English throne, was dead. Most people in England now hailed her half-sister Elizabeth as Queen. However, when Elizabeth was born, Henry VIII's divorced first wife was still alive. To many Catholics, and to others too, Elizabeth was illegitimate and therefore could not be Queen. They regarded Mary Queen of Scots as Queen of England too. For Mary's grandmother had been sister to King Henry VIII.

However, Mary had enough worries of her own. Francis became King of France when his father was killed in a jousting accident. After a year, he too died. Mary, Queen of France no more, decided to return home. She wept when she arrived. It was wet and foggy, and the Palace of Holyroodhouse looked grimmer for not having been used for many years. Scotland was torn by religious differences. The reformers, led by John Knox, had won the battle to make the country Protestant. Catholic mass was forbidden. Churches were vandalised. Yet, much helped by her half-brother, Lord James Stewart (she later made him Earl of Moray), Mary was a good ruler. Though she insisted on having mass in her private chapel, she allowed people to worship as they wished. Then she fell in love with her cousin Lord Darnley, and married him.

Darnley was vain and violent, and unsuitable to share the royal power. He grew jealous, particularly of Mary's secretary, David Rizzio. One night as Mary dined in her apartment with Rizzio and a few special friends, Darnley appeared. A place was made for him at the table. Suddenly a figure with a sword entered the tiny room from the secret staircase which came up from Darnley's bedroom: then more, until the place was filled with armed men. They dragged Rizzio, screaming, outside. Then they stabbed him to death.

When Mary's son James was born, she seemed to be friendly to her husband again. She went to see him in Glasgow, where he was lying ill. She brought him back and lodged him just outside Edinburgh. One night, after she had visited him, an enormous explosion blew the house apart. Darnley's body was found outside. He had been strangled!

Chief suspect of the murder was the Earl of Bothwell. For had not Mary been particularly loving towards him? Bothwell was put on trial but, to everyone's surprise, was found not guilty. And then he and Mary were married! This was too much for most of the Scottish nobles. They raised an army against their Queen. Bothwell escaped. Mary surrendered and was shut up in Lochleven Castle, a prisoner. A month later, they forced her to give up her crown to her little son James.

Mary was Queen no longer, but she still had supporters. Though Lochleven Castle is on an island in a lake, after $10\frac{1}{2}$ months she was free! It is said that she was helped to escape by a page, Willie Douglas. While serving supper, Willie cleverly dropped a napkin over the keys of the Castle, which were lying on the table by the Governor's hand, and went off with them. Plans had already been made. Mary, dressed as a serving girl, was hurried out of the gate, which was locked again behind them. A boat was ready. On shore, a party of Mary's friends was waiting with horses to take her to safety.

Mary was free for only two weeks. Her army was beaten. She fled to England and threw herself on the mercy of her cousin, Queen Elizabeth. But Elizabeth was not going to be kind to someone whom many still believed to be the rightful Queen of England. Mary was shut up in one castle after another, for 19 years. Then in 1587 she was pronounced guilty of plotting to kill Elizabeth. Brave to the last, she was taken down from her room to the great hall of Fotheringay Castle, and there she was beheaded.

Before Mary's death, her two executioners begged her forgiveness. Then, her ladies helped her off with her black gown, under which she had put on a bright red undergarment, so that the blood would not show.

James VI

(1567–1625)

James VI, son of Mary Queen of Scots and of Lord Darnley, was born in the little odd-shaped room in Edinburgh Castle known as Queen Mary's Room. Mary held up the baby and said: 'This is the Prince who, I hope, will first unite the kingdoms of Scotland and England.' Then all the Castle guns were fired, and bonfires were lit.

James never knew his father or his mother. He was only a year old when Mary gave up the throne and went to imprisonment in England. At his coronation at Stirling three Earls bore the royal crown, the sceptre and the sword, while the Earl of Mar carried the baby King in his arms. The country was soon in chaos. James's supporters, known as the King's Lords, fought against the Queen's Lords, who wanted Mary back. At one point there were two Parliaments, one for each side. When James was five, he was made solemnly to attend his Parliament. Bored with what was happening, he asked: 'What is this place?' 'It is Parliament,' he was told. Seeing a tear in the cloth on the table in front of him, and putting his finger through it, James observed: 'Then this Parliament has a hole in it.'

In ten years Scotland had four Regents. Two of them were assassinated by shooting; the third died. Under the fourth, the hated Earl of Morton, the Queen's Lords were crushed, but he too died as violently as many of his enemies. In 1581 James was persuaded to have Morton tried and beheaded for helping to murder Lord Darnley 14 years before. In 1582 three Earls kidnapped the King and ruled in his name for a whole year until he managed to escape.

James was always short of money. The nobles had taken many lands which belonged to the Crown, and of those that he had, James gave some away. When he came back with his bride, the Danish Princess Anne, he had to ask his cousin Queen Elizabeth for money to buy new dinner plates. James could only wait, and wait, for the message from London that would tell him that Elizabeth was dead and that he, her nearest living relative and next in royal line to her, was King too of England.

On 26 March 1603, when James was in bed, a desperately tired horseman rode into the courtyard of the Palace of Holyroodhouse and was taken straight to the royal bedroom. He was Sir Robert Carey and he had ridden the 397 miles from London in sixty hours. Elizabeth was dead, and to prove it he had brought a ring which James had once given to her.

James was now James I of England as well as James VI of Scotland. His money worries were over. With his Queen and his court he moved to London, and he only returned to Scotland once more in his life. However, he continued to govern Scotland through a Privy Council, which passed on his wishes to Parliament. On one very important thing he remained firm. The Scottish Protestants believed that in all religious matters their General Assembly was supreme, even over the King. James replied that the King was Head of the Church and that the Church must be governed by bishops appointed by the King. This bitter argument caused strife and terrible slaughter for many years after James's death.

James was ungainly, and he shuffled along instead of walking. He was an enormous and rather disgusting eater and, because his tongue was unusually large, he made noises when he drank, which was frequently. He never washed his hands and he wore his clothes till they dropped to pieces. His appearance was made odder because he sensibly wore padded coats and breeches in case anyone tried to stab him. When he was young, someone called him 'the Wisest Fool in Christendom'. He was certainly not as much of a fool as he looked, and he did many wise things. By cunning rather than force, he controlled his unruly nobles and stopped them killing each other – one day he had them all to a banquet at the Palace and then made them walk up the hill to the Mercat Cross in pairs, each one hand-in-hand with his greatest enemy! He revived a forgotten Act that landowners in each county should elect two of their number to represent them in Parliament. He strengthened the power of Parliament, which in its turn tried to ensure that its laws were kept and that justice was fairly and properly applied. And he was the first Scottish King since Robert III who lived to what in those days was old age!

James VI was fascinated by witchcraft. He wrote a book about it, presided at trials and even watched people being tortured to make them confess. During his reign hundreds of people accused of being witches were burned alive, and their possessions made over to the King.

Charles I
(1625–1649)

Charles I was three when his father James VI moved to London. He was a sickly child who did not walk until he was seven, and spoke with a stammer. However, when he succeeded James, he had become an excellent sportsman and scholar, and a collector of fine pictures. He was also very religious and believed strongly in a church ruled by bishops, with the King at its Head. This was totally unacceptable to the Scots. He tried too to control the English Parliament and, when he failed, went to war against them. For this, Parliament had him beheaded.

Charles came to Edinburgh for his Scottish coronation in 1633, and the way in which it was celebrated showed the Scots that he did not approve of their Presbyterianism. Then in 1637 he ordered the English style of church service to be used in Scotland too. When it was first read, stools, sticks, stones and bibles were thrown. Riots followed. The National Covenant was drawn up and signed. Its supporters, known as Covenanters, committed themselves to fight for their own kind of worship. In 1640 the Scottish Parliament abolished church rule by bishops and said that the King was no longer Head of the Church in Scotland. To show they meant this, they sent an army into England, which captured Newcastle and Durham.

Though Charles made all sorts of promises, the Scots were not satisfied. They wanted Presbyterianism established in England as well. Charles was now at war with the English Parliament. The Scots came in on the Parliament side and helped to defeat the King's forces at Marston Moor, near York.

The main Scottish army stayed on in England, but now the King's general in Scotland, the Marquis of Montrose, had raised a force of Highlanders which won battle after battle against the Covenanters. However, the final defeat of the King's army at Naseby meant that the Scottish troops in England could go to fight Montrose. He too was defeated. The King asked the Scots for protection. When he still would not agree to establish Presbyterianism in England, they handed him over to the English Parliament, not knowing he might be executed.

Charles II
(1649–1685)

Oliver Cromwell

The Scots were horrified that their King had been executed. Matters were made worse when Oliver Cromwell, who now ruled England for her Parliament, came north and easily defeated them at Dunbar in 1650. The Scots invited Charles I's son to come to Scotland from his exile in Holland. Before he landed the Covenanters made him sign their Covenant and agree to their demands. Then he was crowned King Charles II of Scotland. He took command of the Scottish army and led it into England to try and win back that country too. Cromwell pursued them. At Worcester, in spite of great bravery by the Scots, who were outnumbered two to one, and by Charles himself, Cromwell had a total victory. One of the few to escape was Charles, who managed to reach France after many hair-raising adventures.

The rule of England by Parliament did not last long after Cromwell's death in 1658. In 1660 Charles was restored to the English throne. In Scotland there were great celebrations too – the Edinburgh magistrates gave a street banquet and subscribed £1000 as a gift to the King. But Charles went back on the promise he made in 1650. Bishops were appointed once again. The Covenanters rose up and took the field. Even after their army was finally beaten at Bothwell Brig by the King's illegitimate son, the Duke of Monmouth, many of them would not give up, but continued guerilla war.

Then in 1681 the Scottish Parliament accepted the Test Act, whereby all church ministers and anyone who held office must acknowledge the King as Head of the Church and make no attempt to make any changes in church or government. No Presbyterian minister could accept this. Those that refused never to preach again were thrown into prison.

Charles died at 54. The magnificence of the Palace of Holyroodhouse we owe to him. Much of it was destroyed by fire in 1650. Charles inspected all the plans for its rebuilding and made many suggestions. But though his brother James, Duke of York, lived in the Palace from 1679 to 1682 as Commissioner for Scotland, Charles never set foot in it himself.

James VII – James II of England
(1685–1688)

James revived the Order of the Thistle, which had originally been founded by James V. Today, on special occasions, the Queen and the 16 members of the Order still wear the cloak and badges. The Thistle, as the emblem of Scotland, first appeared on coins in 1474, in the reign of James III.

Charles II and his wife had no children. The heir to the throne was therefore his brother James. As Lord High Admiral from 1660 to 1673, James had shown great naval skill and bravery. In one action against the Dutch, a cannon shot killed three men standing by him, and the head of one of them flew off and knocked him down. James got up and resumed his post, where he stayed for 18 hours until the battle was won. He married Anne Hyde in 1659: they had two daughters, Mary and Anne. Mary later married the Dutch Prince William, who was the son of James's sister and a grandson of Charles I.

After Anne died, James became a Catholic convert and married the 14-year-old Italian Princess, Mary of Modena. The fact that he wanted all his subjects to be Catholics too alarmed many people in England as much as it did the Scots. Harsh measures against Covenanters were increased – it was now punishable by death to preach at or even attend a religious meeting, though those who did not feel they could give up their extreme beliefs were given two months to leave the country.

Even so, James's governments in England and Scotland firmly supported him at the start, and rebellions in Scotland by the Earl of Argyll and in England by the Duke of Monmouth were put down and their leaders executed. Then in 1687 James granted freedom of public worship to everyone. However, this was to prepare the way for establishing Catholicism as a national religion. When he appointed Catholics as judges and to top government and army posts, leading people in England decided that James had gone too far. They invited the Protestant Prince William to come and be King instead, with his wife, James's daughter Mary, as Queen. William landed at Torbay with an army. James now lost his courage, and fled. His disguise was so bad that he was recognised by sailors at the coast and had to return to London, where he was guarded by Dutch soldiers. Obviously they had orders to let him escape, for he got away to France, where he joined his wife and the baby son to whom she had given birth just before she left England.

William and Mary

(1689–1702)   *(1689–1694)*

With James gone, the English offered their crown to William and Mary. The Scots did the same. However, some people still supported James. John Graham of Claverhouse, Viscount Dundee, rode out into the Highlands with his troop of horse. When he was next heard of, he was at the head of an army of Highlanders. Government troops went after him. Dundee waited for them above the Pass of Killiecrankie. The battle was a complete victory for the Highlanders, but at its height a bullet killed Dundee. Without a leader, the Highlanders dispersed.

William was a good statesman, but a hard person whose main amusement was riding. He allowed the establishment at last of the Church of Scotland, governed by its General Assembly, though there were still many people who preferred the English style of worship which James had favoured.

Most Highlanders were still faithful to James too, and refused to sign an Oath of Allegiance to William until they had James's permission to do so. Permission came only a few days before the deadline for signing. Macdonald of Glencoe was late because he had gone to the wrong place and then got caught in a snowstorm. A month later, thirty members of his clan were massacred by troops of the King.

William agreed to abolish rule of Scotland through a Privy Council and to let Parliament do the governing. To get trade for their desperately poor country, the Scots proposed to found a colony at Darien, on the isthmus of Panama. William did not help because he could not do so without harming English interests or offending Spain, which laid claim to the land on which Darien stood. The scheme failed, with the loss of many Scottish lives and much Scottish money.

After Mary died childless, William ruled alone. One day his horse stumbled over a mole-hill and threw him. William broke his collar-bone and died a few days later. Few people in Scotland mourned him. Indeed Jacobites, as the supporters of James were known, raised their glasses to 'the little gentleman in black velvet' – the mole which had caused William's fall.

What Happened Next

James Edward Stuart, son of James VII and father of Bonnie Prince Charlie, was known as the Old Pretender. All his attempts to gain the throne failed.

George IV

When James VII died in France in 1701, the Jacobites regarded his son by his second marriage, James Edward Stuart, as now the rightful King of England and Scotland. However, on William's death, the Protestant Anne, daughter of James VII by Anne Hyde and younger sister of Mary, was crowned Queen. Her reign was memorable for success in the wars in Europe, for literature, art and architecture. It also brought the Union of the English and Scottish Parliaments. Britain now had one monarch and one Parliament, and both were in London. Though Scotland had lost control of her own affairs, there were advantages too. Now Scottish merchants could trade where before only the English had been allowed to go. Glasgow was the nearest port in Britain to the rich markets in America and the West Indies, and many of her merchants soon became very prosperous.

Anne was married to Prince George of Denmark. Though she had 17 children, only one survived infancy and he died in 1700. On Anne's death in 1714, there was no-one left from the original Stewart line to succeed her. So, as James V prophesied, the line did 'end with a lass'. Anne's nearest Protestant relation was her cousin George, grandson of James VII. He was a German prince who spoke no English. Yet he became King George I of Great Britain, and his descendants have ruled Britain ever since.

However, in the very next year the Earl of Mar raised the banner of James Edward Stuart in the Highlands and publicly proclaimed him the true King. After a battle at Sheriffmuir which neither side really won, the rebellion fizzled out, and James Edward himself did not arrive until it was too late. The next big excitement was in 1745. James Edward's son Charles (Bonnie Prince Charlie) suddenly appeared in the Highlands and claimed the thrones of England and Scotland for his father. Thousands flocked to join him. He beat the government army and entered Edinburgh in triumph. He invaded England and got within 130 miles of London itself before his officers persuaded him to turn back. He was finally defeated in battle at Culloden Moor and, after many adventures, escaped to France. He never came back to Scotland again.

When George IV came to Edinburgh in 1822, he was the first reigning British monarch to visit Scotland since Charles II over 150 years before. It was a time of pageantry and joy, and also some mirth. The King had been advised to wear full Highland dress, with kilt and short tartan stockings, which he put on over flesh-coloured tights. As he was a very fat man, he presented a strange appearance. One Edinburgh official, seeing a fat man in a kilt, knelt and kissed his hand. Unfortunately it was not the King, but one of his attendants, who had been made to wear kilts too.

Twenty years later Queen Victoria, then aged 23, and her husband Prince Albert, paid a royal visit. Though the crowds were out to welcome her, the officials who were meant to meet her on the outskirts of Edinburgh and present her with the keys of the city, were still having breakfast when she arrived. So the royal carriage swept on through the city and out to Dalkeith, where the Queen was to stay. When the officials heard this, they jumped into their carriages and set off in pursuit, but they could not catch up with her. Further visits were much better organised, and Queen Victoria returned to Scotland again and again. Such was her love for the Highlands that she insisted that her Scottish servant, John Brown, should accompany her everywhere. The publication of her book, *Leaves from the Journal of our Life in the Highlands,* was important in establishing the Scottish tourist industry. The present Balmoral Castle was built as a holiday home for her, and has been regularly used ever since by her successors.

George V made several state visits to Scotland, and it was during his reign that the Palace of Holyroodhouse was repaired and work done on parts of it which had been left unfinished by Charles II's architect. It is now a royal palace again, fit for Victoria's great-great-granddaughter and descendant of Robert the Bruce, HM the Queen Elizabeth, to stay in and hold court in every year.

Queen Victoria, Prince Albert and their two eldest children, the Princess Royal and the Prince of Wales, afterwards Edward VII.

Places to Visit

Balmoral Castle, by Ballater
The grounds are open in the summer when the Royal Family is not there.
Bannockburn Heritage Centre, Stirling
Exhibition and display of the battle: statue of Robert the Bruce.
Blair Castle, by Pitlochry
Home of the Duke of Atholl. Mary Queen of Scots and Bonnie Prince Charlie stayed here, and there are many Jacobite relics.
Dunfermline Abbey, Monastery Street
Includes remains of the ancient church founded by St Margaret, and her shrine. Robert the Bruce is buried here.
Edinburgh Castle
See especially St Margaret's Chapel, the Great Hall built by James IV, Queen Mary's Room, and the Regalia of Scotland.
Falkland Palace
James V died in the King's Bed Chamber, and Mary Queen of Scots spent much time here both as a child and when she was grown up. Splendid gardens.
Linlithgow Palace
Birthplace of Mary Queen of Scots. Fine 15th-century ruin.
Palace of Holyroodhouse, Edinburgh
Official residence of HM the Queen in Scotland. James IV built the north-west tower in which are the apartments of Mary Queen of Scots where Rizzio was murdered.
Parliament House, Edinburgh
Meeting place of the Scottish Parliament from 1639 until 1707.
Scone Palace, by Perth
Parts of the building go back to the 16th century. Collections of porcelain, furniture and early clocks and needlework. On the Mote Hill Kenneth I set the ancient Stone of Destiny on which early Scottish Kings were crowned.
Scottish National Portrait Gallery, Queen Street, Edinburgh
Includes portraits of Scottish Kings and Queens.
Stirling Castle
Parts built by James III and James V still remain. Home of Scottish Kings and for many years the main seat of government.
Tantallon Castle, by North Berwick
Stronghold of the Douglases, besieged by James V. A ruin since Cromwell's invasion of Scotland.
Traquair House, by Peebles
Many Scottish Kings and Queens stayed here, including Mary Queen of Scots, of whom there are relics on display. It is said that the main gates were locked after a visit by Bonnie Prince Charlie, and are never to be opened again until a Stuart returns to the throne.

For further details about these and other places to visit, including opening times, ring Scottish Tourist Board, 031-332 2433, or write to PO Box 705, Edinburgh EH4 3EU.